The Vowel Tree Christmas Tale

Published by Pure Joy Teaching

ISBN: 978-1-7644532-0-2

Copyright © 2025 by D. Passmore

Illustrations © 2025 by D. Passmore

All rights reserved.

purejoyteaching.com

All rights reserved. No part of this publication may be reproduced, distributed, or transmitted in any form or by any means, including photocopying, recording, or other electronic or mechanical methods, without the prior written permission of the publisher, except in the case of brief quotations embodied in critical reviews and certain other noncommercial uses permitted by copyright law.

A told E, and I told U.

"We can make a vowel tree."

"O, O, Oh, don't go…. without me!"

Letter O is excited about the vowel tree.

B, C, D, F, and G say, "We are consonants. We will stay here under the tree."

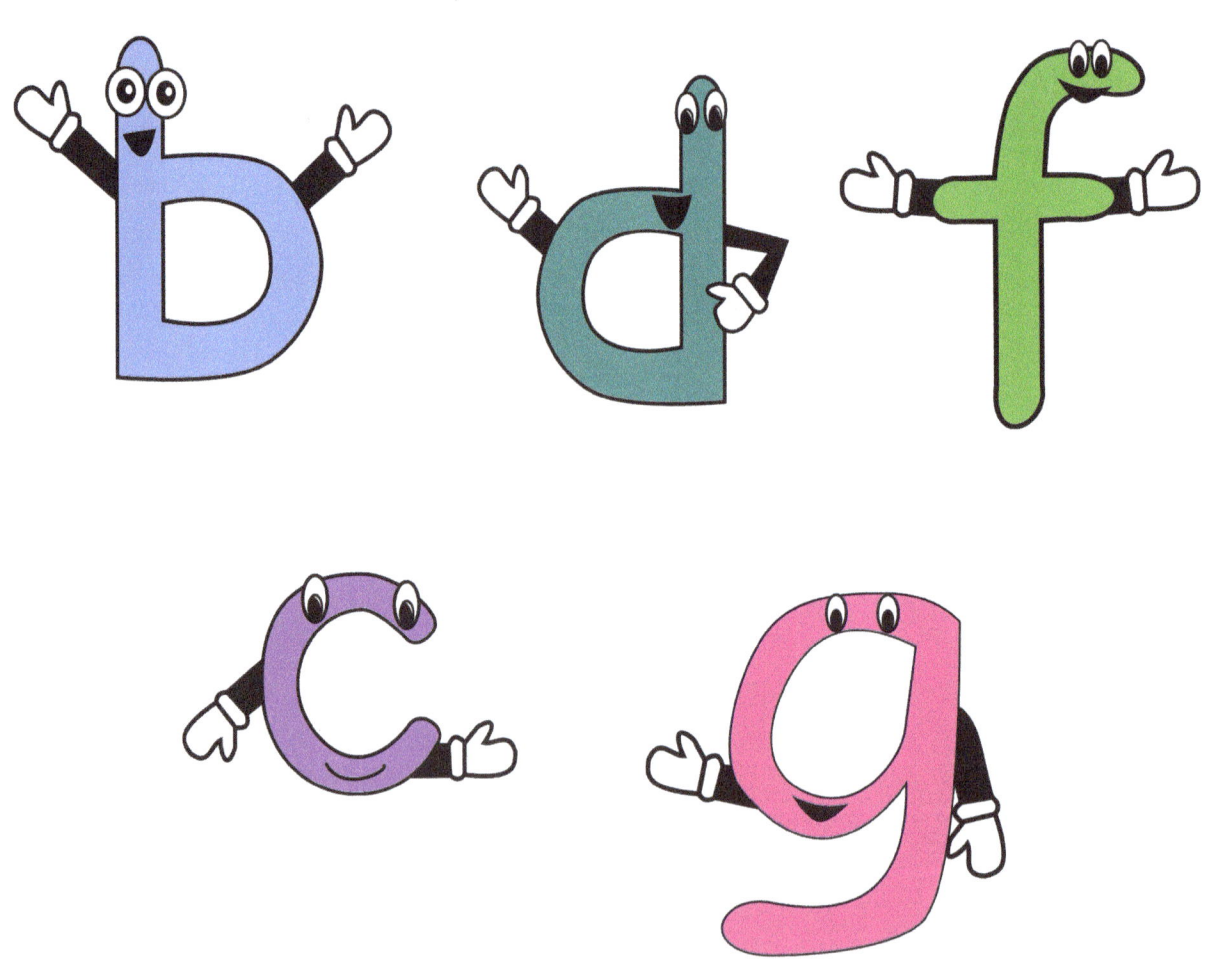

H laughed loud and joked with J, "There is no way five little vowels will fill up that tree."

"E, E, E, Look at me! I can double myself and be the ē sound in tree." E told A, "We are part of a vowel team. If we link together, we can fill up this tree." Together they make the ē sound in team.

Instantly, the letter I announced his idea, "A and I can link together in a chain!" Vowels A & I, they say "A" in the words chain and train.

K shakes L. "Look at that! Those five small vowels are trying to fill up the tree."

L, M, N, and P, Cheer with glee, "The five little vowels can fill up the tree!"

I and E like to tie. They say "I" and make up a vowel team.

U and E help to spell the /oo/ sound in glue and blue. O and O put the /oo/ in moo and the /oo/ in hook. O grabbed U, "We are the /oo/ in group."

U and I put the /oo/ in suit.

Q, R, S, T, celebrate, "These five little vowels can fill up that tree."

E and A have three different sounds. The ē in please, ĕ sound in bread, and the ā in great.

E says to O, "Let's join to be the oh in toe."
A grabs O, "We can say the oh in coat."

A, E, I, O, U sing with glee, "We five little vowels can fill up this tree."

A yells, "Hey, tricky guy Y, come on up and be part of the vowel tree." Together, A and Y say "A."

Letter Y is so tricky that it can be all over the tree.

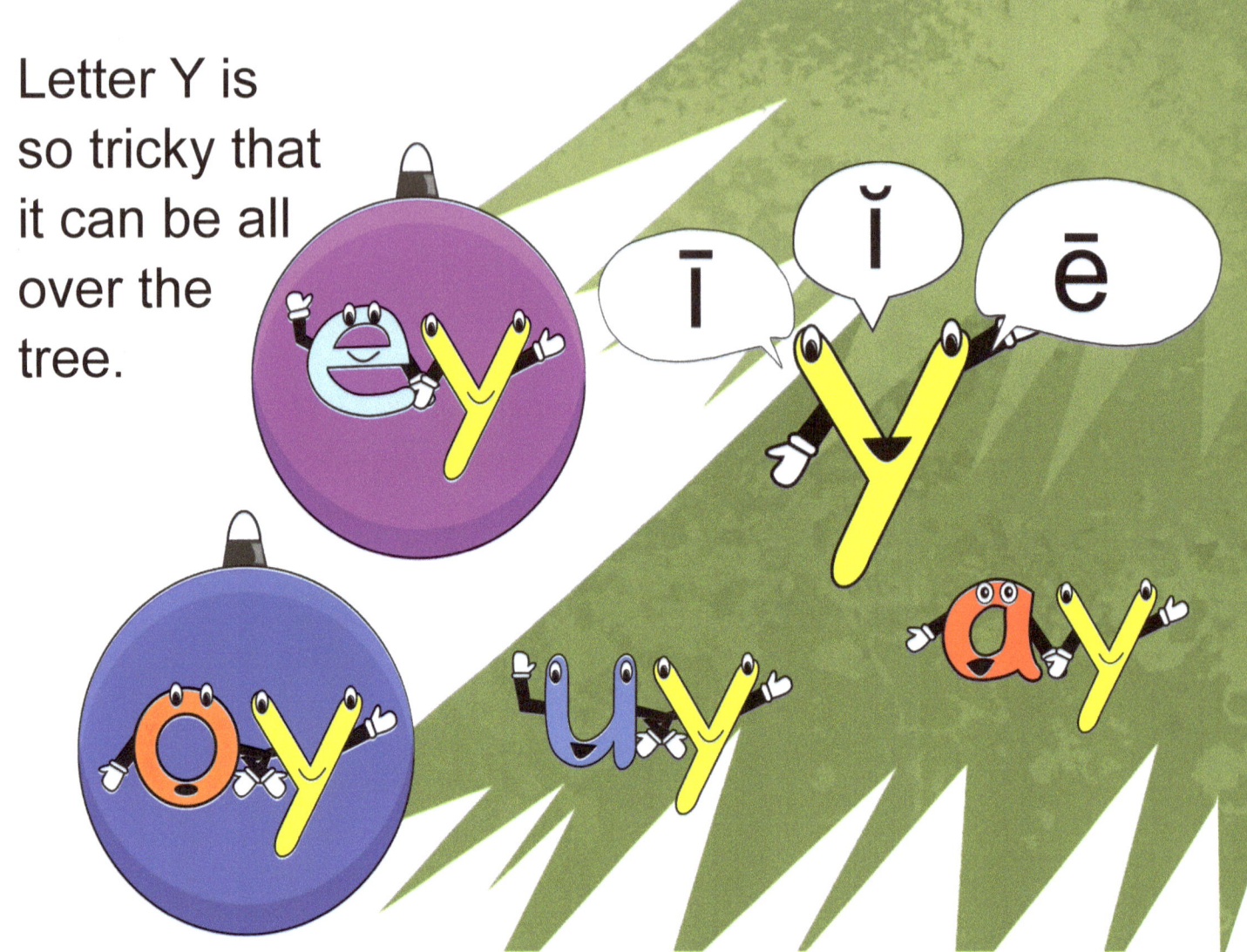

Y is the I in try, the E in happy, and the /i/ in gym.

Y is a silent team player in play, and the E in key.
Y paired with O, it is the /oi/ sound in joy.

U and Y are the tricky I sound in guy.

O grabs I.

We are the /oi/ sound in the middle of coil.

W hops, and yells, "Woe, woe, woe! Oh, what about me?"

Can W work with the vowels to fill up the tree?

O pulls W up and says, "Yes, you know there is still room on the vowel tree.

Together OW, we say oh as in snow."

V waves goodbye from below.

snow

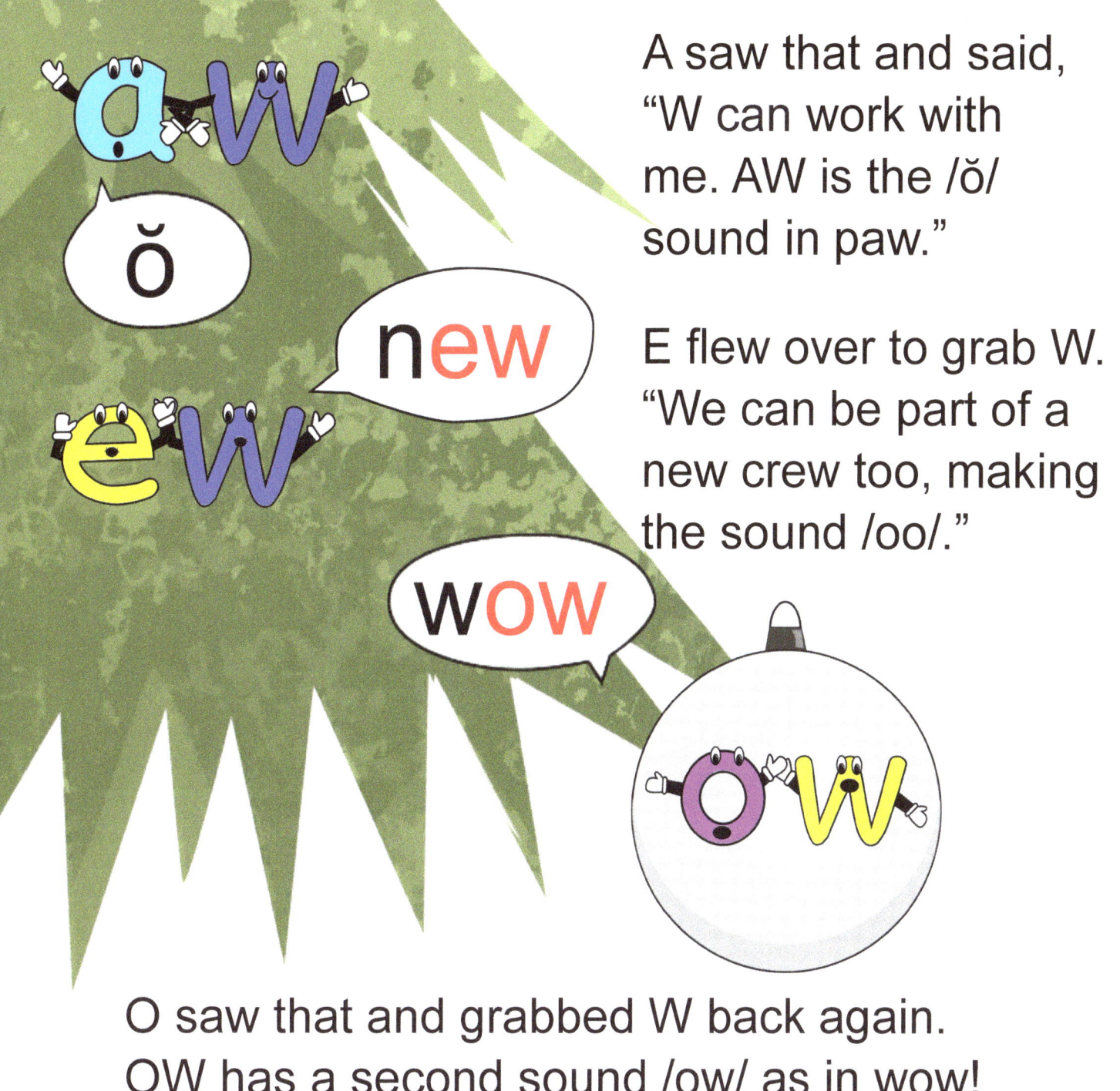

A saw that and said, "W can work with me. AW is the /ŏ/ sound in paw."

E flew over to grab W. "We can be part of a new crew too, making the sound /oo/."

O saw that and grabbed W back again. OW has a second sound /ow/ as in wow!

U reached out to get letter O. "Ouch don't crowd." OU can make the /ou/ as in bounce.

A grabs U and they say, "/ŏ/ that's okay."

A, E, I, O, U sway & twirl. "We five vowels worked together to fill up the vowel tree."

ou ch

ŏ

Everyone, it is time to peek under the tree. Look! G and H are sneaking silently up the tree.

Letter I grabs them quickly and hugs them tight. "You can stay here and say 'I' with me on the vowel tree. We spell the I in lights."

The rest of the consonant letters lay under the tree, basking in the glow of the vowel tree.

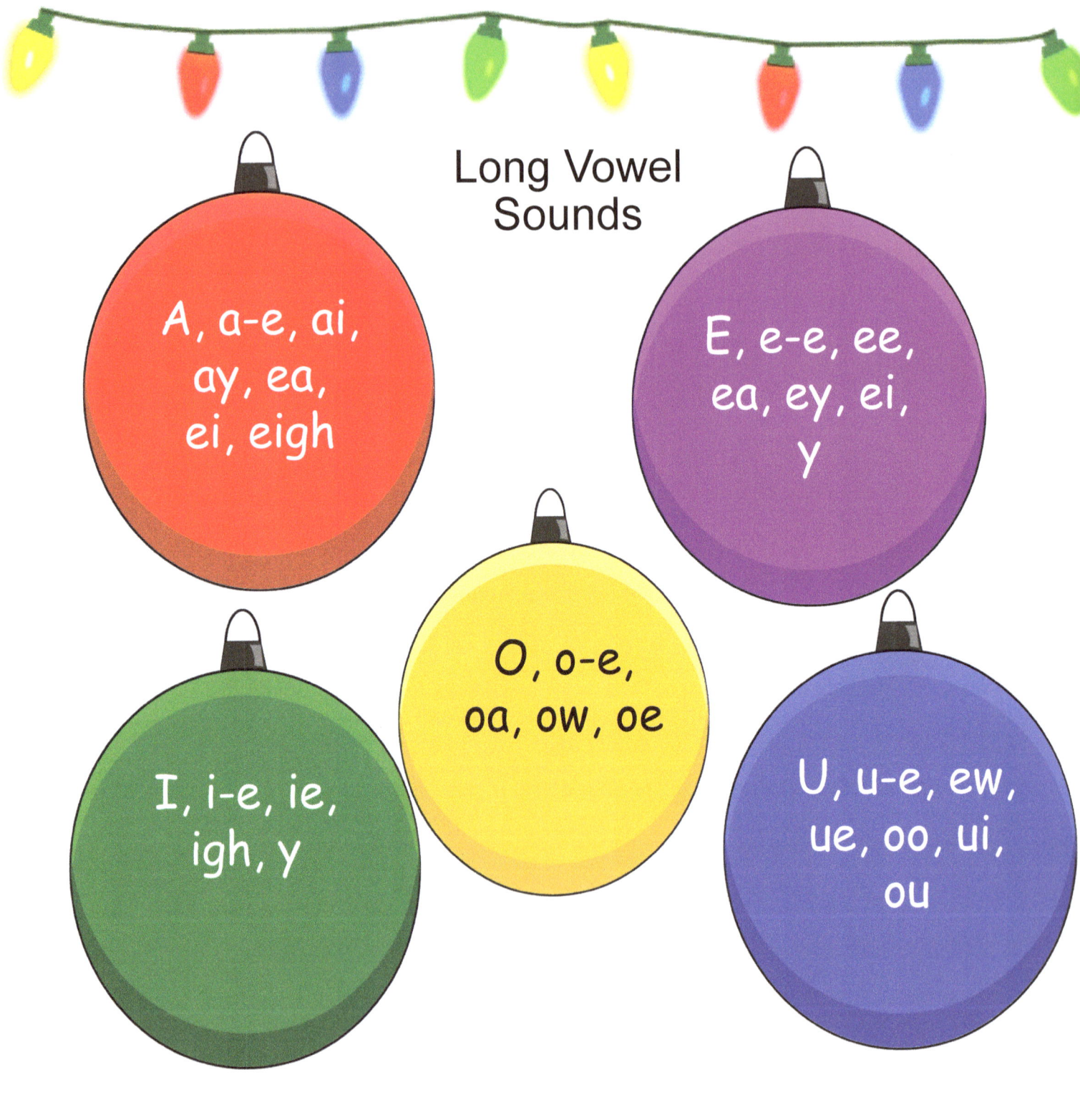

There are 26 letters in the English alphabet. Five of them are vowels: **a, e, i, o,** and **u**. Vowels are special because they can make more than one sound, and they can work together in teams to make new sounds. Every English word needs a vowel or a letter acting like a vowel—sometimes that job is done by the tricky letter y.

Only the five vowels can say their own names in words. This is called the **long vowel sound**. Consonants do **not** say their names in words; they only make their own sounds. Unlike vowels, consonants do not have long and short sounds.

Some consonants can be silent helpers to vowels or can influence the sounds vowels make.

The five short vowel sounds are: ă, ĕ, ĭ, ŏ, ŭ.

www.ingramcontent.com/pod-product-compliance
Lightning Source LLC
Chambersburg PA
CBHW061116070526
44583CB00027B/3314